5 MINUTE
Sunday School Activities
For Preschoolers

Jesus Shows Me

For information regarding the CPSIA on this printed material call:
203-595-3636 and provide reference # LANC-315751

rainbowpublishers®

Rainbow Publishers • P.O. Box 261129 • San Diego, CA 92196
www.RainbowPublishers.com

5 MINUTE

Sunday School Activities

For Preschoolers

Jesus Shows Me

Mary J. Davis

To my husband, Larry, our children and grandchildren.
To my friends, Ann Eaton, Gwen Hanson, Margie Stice.

5 MINUTE SUNDAY SCHOOL ACTIVITIES FOR PRESCHOOLERS: JESUS SHOWS ME
©2011 Rainbow Publishers, sixth printing
ISBN 10: 1-58411-047-3
ISBN 13: 978-1-58411-047-7
Rainbow reorder# RB38412
RELIGION / Christian Ministry / Children

Rainbow Publishers
P.O. Box 261129
San Diego, CA 92196
www.RainbowPublishers.com

Interior Illustrator: Chuck Galey
Cover Illustrator: Todd Marsh

SUSTAINABLE FORESTRY INITIATIVE

Certified Chain of Custody
Promoting Sustainable
Forest Management
www.sfiprogram.org

Scriptures are from the *Holy Bible: New International Version* (North American Edition), ©1973, 1978, 1984 by the International Bible Society. Used by permission of Zondervan Bible Publishers.

Printed in the United States of America

Contents

JESUS TEACHES ME

A Lamp Under a Bushel 9

The Sower and the Seed..........................11

The Weeds and the Wheat......................13

The Mustard Seed 15

The Hidden Treasure 17

The Good and Bad Fish 19

The Lost Sheep 21

The Unmerciful Servant.......................23

The Two Sons......................................25

The Wedding Banquet 27

The Fig Tree 29

The Sheep and the Goats 31

The Talents 33

The Good Samaritan..............................35

The Rich Fool......................................37

The Lost Coin 39

The Lost Son 41

The Growing Seed 43

The Two Debtors..................................45

The Pharisee and Tax Collector 47

Jesus Taught People About God..............49

JESUS SHOWS ME

Jesus Turns Water into Wine 51

The Large Catch of Fish 53

Jesus Calms the Storm 55

Jesus Feeds 5,000 57

Jesus Heals a Nobleman's Son 59

Jesus Heals Peter's Mother-in-Law 61

Jesus Heals a Leper..............................63

Friends Know Jesus Heals.......................65

Jesus Walks on Water 67

The Tax Money 69

Jesus Helps Disciples Catch Fish 71

Jesus Helps a Man Walk.........................73

Jesus Heals a Man's Hand......................75

Jesus Heals a Centurion Servant 77

Jesus Helps a Man to See & Hear............79

Jesus Heals a Little Girl 81

A Woman Touches Jesus' Clothing..........83

Jesus Heals Ten Lepers...........................85

Jesus Heals Blind Bartimaeus 87

Jesus Calls Out Lazarus 89

Jesus Heals a Crippled Woman 91

Jesus Healed Many People 93

Jesus Is the Son of God...........................95

Introduction

Children need to grow up learning about Jesus. Even young preschoolers can begin to grasp the concept of Jesus' love and care for us. Jesus' miracles and parables are wonderful teaching tools. Children will understand that Jesus cares, Jesus loves and Jesus wants them to know about God and heaven.

5-Minute Sunday School Activities for Preschoolers is designed to give teachers a quick activity that teaches an important Bible truth. Teachers are often faced with a few extra minutes after the lesson is finished. There are also times when a teacher needs a few moments to get attendance and other important matters out of the way before the main lesson. Instead of wasting these minutes with non-learning play, provide a 5-minute activity for the children.

The activities in the book can also be used as entire lessons. Scriptures, teaching suggestions and memory verses are included with each activity.

As a teacher of young children, you can make these activities go quickly by doing much of the preparatory work before class. You may also make the activities take longer, by allowing children to do their own cutting.

EXTRA TIME suggestions will be given for the activities. If you have more than 5 minutes for children to complete the craft, you may want to choose the extra time suggestion.

The Weeds and the Wheat
Matthew 13:24-30

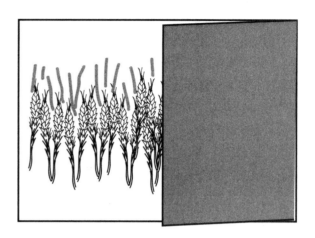

WHAT YOU NEED

- page 14, duplicated
- crayons
- yarn
- glue

BEFORE CLASS

Duplicate a pattern page for each child. Cut several lengths of yarn, around 3-6 inches long, for each child. Make a sample craft to show the children.

WHAT TO DO

1. Introduce the lesson by telling the parable from Matthew 13:24-30. Say, **Even when sin and bad things are in the world, God takes special care to watch over us. We are His children.**
2. Show the children the sample craft.
3. Distribute a pattern page to each child.
4. Say the memory verse.
5. Tell the children to glue some yarn "weeds" among the wheat in the scene. Have the children color the page as time allows. Discuss some things the weeds might represent in the children's lives. Suggest: lying, disobeying parents, not sharing, etc.

EXTRA TIME

Provide a half-sheet of red construction paper for each child. Have the children glue yarn "weeds" to only half of the page. On the other half, have the children tape the red construction paper, as shown, to represent a barn.

lue some weeds in the picture of wheat. Remember that Jesus said the weeds would be burned, and the wheat would be stored safely in the barn.

14

The Mustard Seed
Mark 4:30-32

Jesus said the mustard seed
Is smallest of them all.
But when it's planted in the ground,
It becomes a tree, grand and tall.
Jesus told this story
So that we could see
How marvelous and wonderful,
How grand heaven will be.

WHAT YOU NEED

- page 16, duplicated
- crayons
- mustard seeds
- glue

BEFORE CLASS

Duplicate a pattern page for each child. Make a sample craft to show the children.

WHAT TO DO

1. Introduce the lesson by telling the parable from Mark 4:30-32. Say, **Jesus tells us that a mustard seed is very tiny. From it grows a tall, beautiful tree that birds can sit in. Jesus says that heaven is like that. It is beautiful and wonderful.**
2. Show the children the sample craft.
3. Distribute a pattern page to each child.
4. Say the memory verse.
5. Have the children color the tree poster.
6. Help the students glue a mustard seed onto the page.
7. Read the poem to the children.

EXTRA TIME

Show pictures of real trees, or take the children outdoors to see how tall some trees are. Let each child hold a mustard seed and compare it to a tree picture or a real tree.

olor a tree poster and add a tiny mustard
seed. Compare the seed to the tree to see
how wonderful heaven will be.

Jesus said the mustard seed
Is smallest of them all.
But when it's planted in the ground,
It becomes a tree, grand and tall.
Jesus told this story
So that we could see
How marvelous and wonderful,
How grand heaven will be.

The Hidden Treasure
Matthew 13:44

MEMORY VERSE

The kingdom of heaven is like treasure.
~ Matthew 13:44

WHAT YOU NEED

- page 18, duplicated
- crayons

BEFORE CLASS

Duplicate a pattern page for each child. Show a sample craft to the children if you desire. You may not want to show the page to older preschoolers, so they may discover the treasures themselves.

WHAT TO DO

1. Introduce the lesson by telling about the hidden treasure from Matthew 13:44. Say, **Jesus says that heaven will be wonderful, just like a hidden treasure.**
2. Show the children the sample page, if you desire.
3. Distribute a pattern page to each child.
4. Say the memory verse.
5. Tell the children to find and circle the 11 treasure boxes hidden in the picture. The children may color the picture as time allows. Say, **A treasure is something very special. Heaven also will be very special.**

EXTRA TIME

Have the children find and circle the treasure boxes. Then give each child 11 foil or gold stickers (or 1-inch square pieces of foil) to glue onto the treasure boxes. Stress that heaven will be a wonderful place.

Find the hidden treasures in the picture. Think of how wonderful heaven will be.

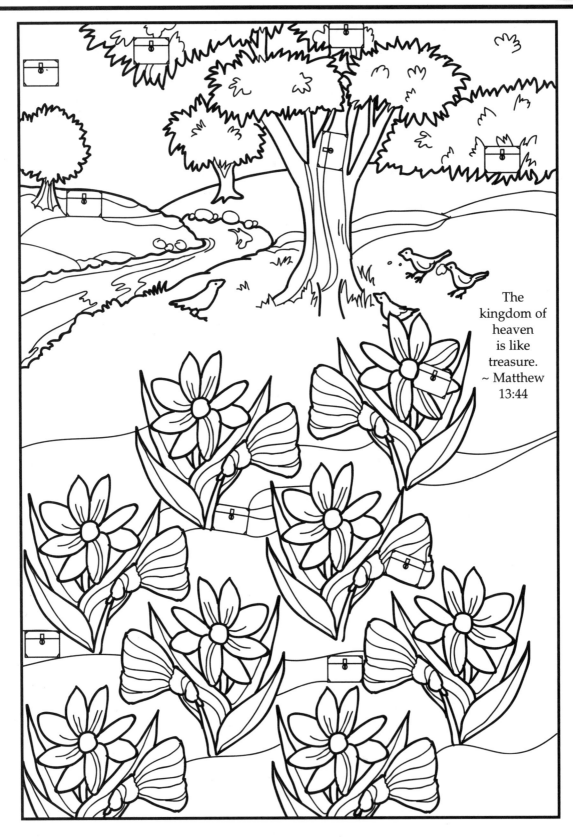

The kingdom of heaven is like treasure.
~ Matthew 13:44

The Good and Bad Fish
Matthew 13:47-49

MEMORY VERSE

The angels will come and separate the wicked [bad] from the righteous [good].
~ Matthew 13:49

WHAT YOU NEED

- page 20, duplicated
- crayons
- tape
- hole punch
- yarn

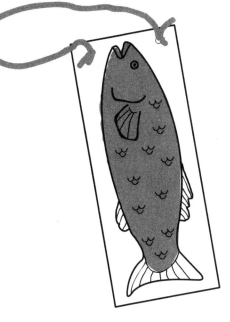

BEFORE CLASS

Duplicate a pattern page for each child. Cut a two-foot length of yarn for each child. Make a sample craft to show the children.

WHAT TO DO

1. Introduce the lesson by telling about the parable from Matthew 13:47-49. Say, **Jesus says that angels will sort out the good from the bad people like the fisherman picked the good fish and threw out the bad fish.**
2. Show the children the sample craft.
3. Distribute a pattern page to each child.
4. Say the memory verse.
5. Allow the students to color the fish windsock.
6. Have the children fold the page on the dashed line, then tape the seam.
7. Help the children punch two holes at the front end of the windsock, then tie the yarn through each hole to form a hanger. Say, **When you hang up your windsock at home, you will be reminded that God's people are like the good fish.**

EXTRA TIME

Provide sequins, round cereal pieces or miniature marshmallows for the children to glue onto the fish for textured scales.

esus tells about a net that catches all the fish.
Angels will sort out the good fish from the bad.
Make a fish windsock to remember this parable.

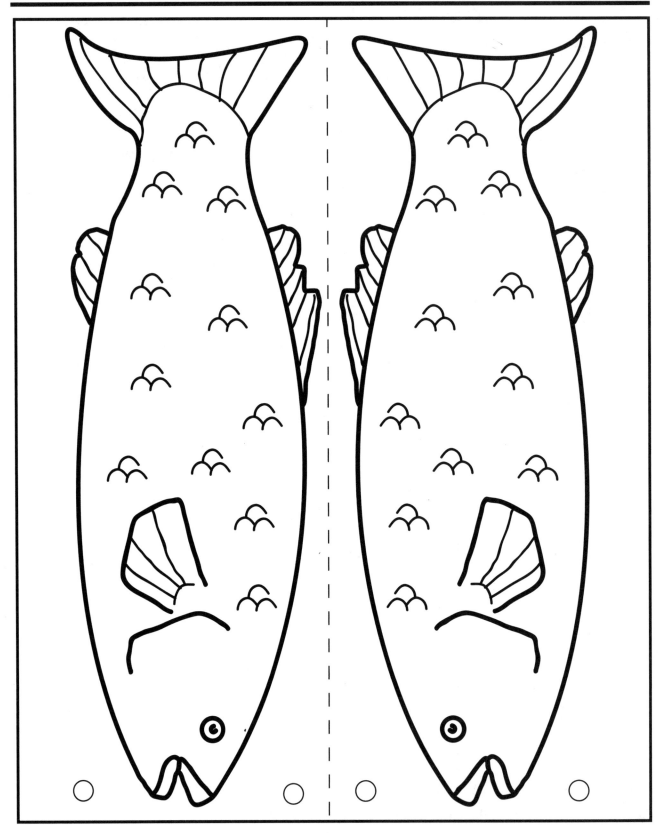

The Lost Sheep
Luke 15:3-7

MEMORY VERSE

Rejoice...I have found my lost sheep.
~ Luke 15:6

WHAT YOU NEED

- page 22, duplicated
- crayons
- safety scissors

BEFORE CLASS

Duplicate a pattern page for each child. For younger children, cut out the five rectangular figures. Make a sample craft to show the children.

WHAT TO DO

1. Introduce the lesson by telling the story of the lost sheep. Use the sample craft to tell the story. Say, **God loves each of us very much. If we aren't following God, we are like lost sheep. But when we are following God, all of heaven is happy.**
2. Distribute a sample page to each child.
3. Say the memory verse.
4. Have the children cut out the five rectangular figures on the bold lines and fold each on the dashed lines to stand up.
5. Have the children color their stand-up figures.
6. Retell the story while children play with their stand-up figures. Have the children hug the lone sheep. Say, **God is happy when He finds His lost sheep.**

EXTRA TIME

Provide cotton balls for the children to glue onto the sheep figures.

ake a stand-up scene to tell the
parable of the lost sheep.

Luke 15:3-7

The Unmerciful Servant
Matthew 18:23-35

MEMORY VERSE

Forgive your brother from your heart.
~ Matthew 18:35

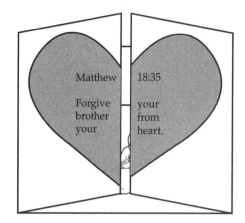

WHAT YOU NEED

- page 24, duplicated
- crayons
- safety scissors

BEFORE CLASS

Duplicate a pattern page for each child. For younger preschoolers, cut the two squares from the bottom corners of the page. Make the folds for the children. Make a sample craft to show the children.

WHAT TO DO

1. Introduce the lesson by telling the parable from Matthew 18:23-35. Say, **The servant was forgiven. But he would not forgive someone else. God wants us to forgive others.**
2. Show the children the sample craft.
3. Distribute a pattern page to each child.
4. Say the memory verse.
5. Have the children cut the corners from the page, cutting on the solid lines.
6. Help the children fold the flaps all toward the center of the page. The heart flaps should be on the outside with the other flap inside as a pocket.
7. Have the children color the pictures as time allows. Talk about each picture while the children work.
8. Show how to slip the picture squares into the pocket. Discuss situations when the children might need to forgive others. Suggest: broken toy, argument, hurt feelings, not sharing.

EXTRA TIME

Have the children color the heart on the front of the pocket story. Tape the sides of the pocket to make the craft more sturdy. Have the children retell the story, using their pocket stories.

ake a "pocket" picture to tell
about the servant who was
forgiven, then would not forgive.

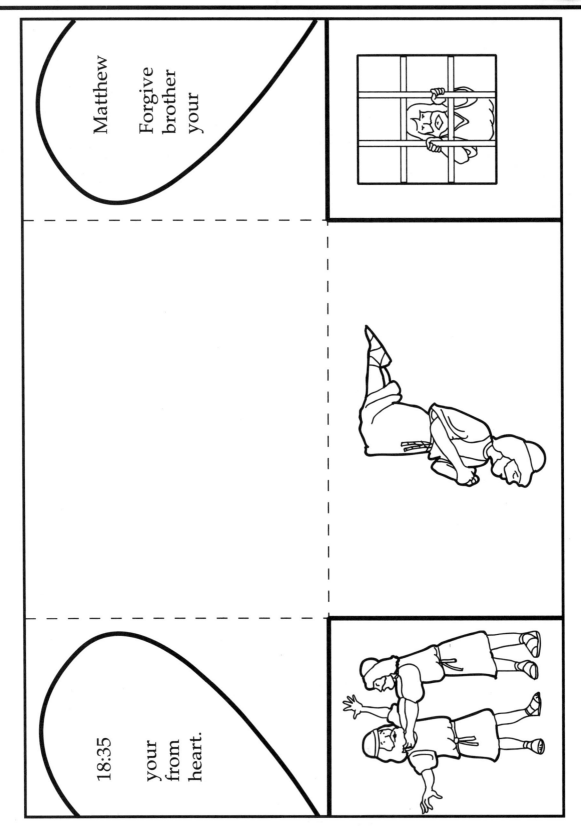

Matthew

Forgive
brother
your

18:35

your
from
heart.

The Two Sons
Matthew 21:28-32

MEMORY VERSE

And even after you saw this, you did not...believe.
~ Matthew 21:32

WHAT YOU NEED

- page 26, duplicated
- crayons
- tape
- yarn

BEFORE CLASS

Duplicate a pattern page for each child. Cut an 8" length of yarn for each child. Make a sample craft to show the children.

WHAT TO DO

1. Introduce the lesson by telling the parable from Matthew 21:28-32. Say, **One son said he would go into the vineyard to work, but he didn't. One son said he wouldn't go, but he did. Sometimes God's people say they will do things for God, but then they don't. God wants us to be willing to do His work.**
2. Show the children the sample craft.
3. Distribute a pattern page to each child.
4. Say the memory verse.
5. Have the children fold the page in half. Tape at the seam.
6. Tape the yarn at the top for a hanger.
7. Have the children color both sides of the plaque as time allows. Retell the story as the children work. Discuss things we can do to work for God. Suggest: help others, tell others about God, help at church, etc.

EXTRA TIME

Duplicate the page onto card stock. Have the children complete the craft as above. Then provide pasta pieces for the children to glue around the edges for a textured frame.

M
ake a story plaque to tell
about the two sons.

A man told his sons to go and work in the vineyard. The first son said, "I will not go." But later, he went.

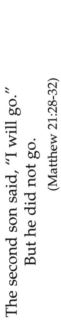

The second son said, "I will go." But he did not go. (Matthew 21:28-32)

And even after you saw this, you did not...believe.
~ Matthew 21:32

The Fig Tree
Luke 21:29-33

MEMORY VERSE

My words will never pass away.
~ Luke 21:33

Look at the fig trees

...know that ...near

WHAT YOU NEED

- page 30, duplicated
- crayons

BEFORE CLASS

Duplicate a pattern page for each child. Make a sample craft to show the children.

WHAT TO DO

1. Introduce the lesson by telling the parable from Luke 21:29-33. Say, **Trees begin to bud with tiny leaves. Then the leaves get big and green, and the tree is beautiful. In the fall, leaves fall off the tree and dry up. Jesus wants us to know His words will never go away like the leaves on the trees.**
2. Show the children the sample craft.
3. Distribute a pattern page to each child.
4. Say the memory verse.
5. Help the children fold the page on the broken lines, as shown.
6. While the children color the page, discuss the stages of the tree. Show a Bible to demonstrate what the "Word" is.

EXTRA TIME

Show a fig, or allow the children to taste a fig, as you tell the parable. Show pictures of trees and leaves in different seasons. If possible, bring green leaves and dried leaves. Allow the children to crumble the dry leaves.

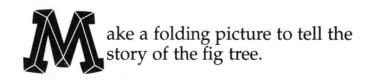

Make a folding picture to tell the story of the fig tree.

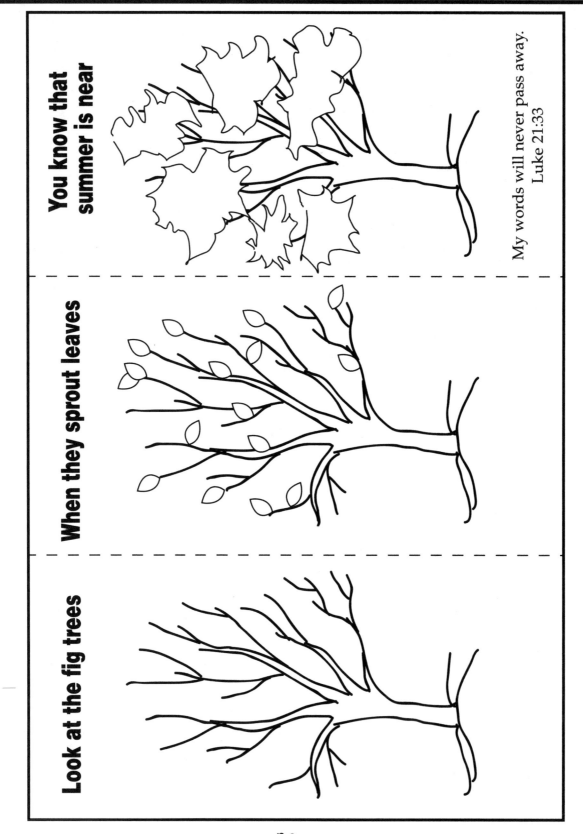

You know that summer is near

My words will never pass away.
Luke 21:33

When they sprout leaves

Look at the fig trees

The Sheep and the Goats

Matthew 25:31-46

He will put the sheep on his right and the goats on his left.
Matthew 25:33

WHAT YOU NEED

- page 32, duplicated
- crayons

BEFORE CLASS

Duplicate a pattern page for each child. Make a sample craft to show the children. For older preschoolers, do not complete the picture–allow the children to discover the picture themselves.

WHAT TO DO

1. Introduce the lesson by telling about the sheep and goats from Matthew 25:31-46. Say, **In heaven, Jesus will separate people like a shepherd separates sheep from goats. The good people, those who love Jesus, will stay in heaven.**
2. Show the children the sample craft.
3. Distribute a pattern page to each child.
4. Say the memory verse.
5. Tell the children to connect the dots to discover what is on the page. Then have the children color the sheep and goats, as time allows. Discuss the idea of separating good from bad. Stress that the sheep are those who follow Jesus.

EXTRA TIME

Provide cotton balls and craft sticks. Have the children glue the cotton on the sheep and the craft sticks on the posts of the throne.

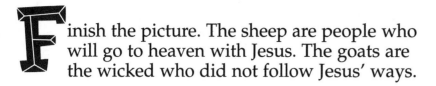
Finish the picture. The sheep are people who will go to heaven with Jesus. The goats are the wicked who did not follow Jesus' ways.

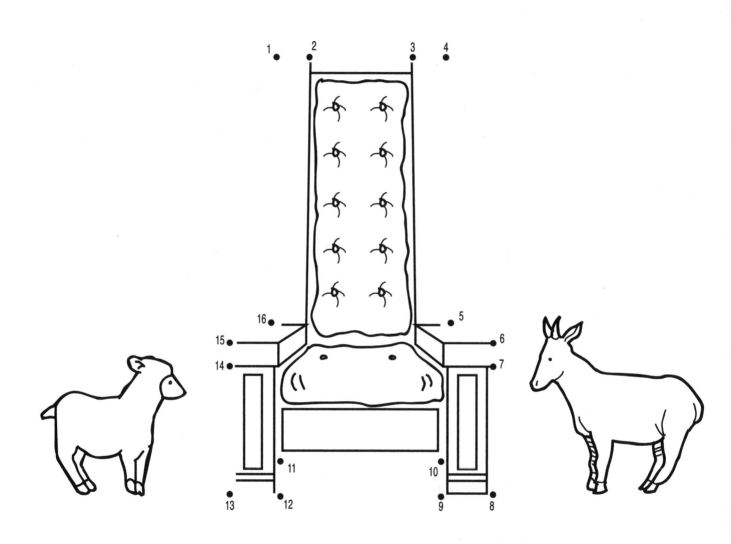

He will put the sheep on his right and the goats on his left.
Matthew 25:33

The Talents
Matthew 25:14-30

WHAT YOU NEED

- page 34, duplicated
- crayons
- safety scissors
- yarn
- hole punch
- tape

BEFORE CLASS

Duplicate a pattern page for each child. For younger preschoolers, cut out the simple pieces. Punch holes in the folded pouch. Cut a one-foot length of yarn for each child. Make a sample craft to show the children.

WHAT TO DO

1. Introduce the lesson by telling the parable in Matthew 25:14-30. Say, **Jesus wants us to use our talents to serve Him. Everyone has a way to serve Jesus.**
2. Show the children the sample craft.
3. Distribute a pattern page to each child.
4. Say the memory verse.
5. Have the children cut out the simple pieces.
6. Have the children fold the pouch on the fold line. Tape the sides.
7. Help the students thread a one-foot length of yarn through the holes and tie at the front.
8. Have the children slip the talent strips inside the pouch.
9. The children may color the craft as time allows. Discuss each talent card. Ask the children to tell ways they can use each talent.

EXTRA TIME

Have a "talent" show. Allow the children to sing, tell a Bible story, tell a joke, etc. Say, **Everyone has a way to serve Jesus. You all have great talents!**

H ow do you use the talents God gave you? See how some men used their talents in this parable. Make a pouch in which to keep your talents.

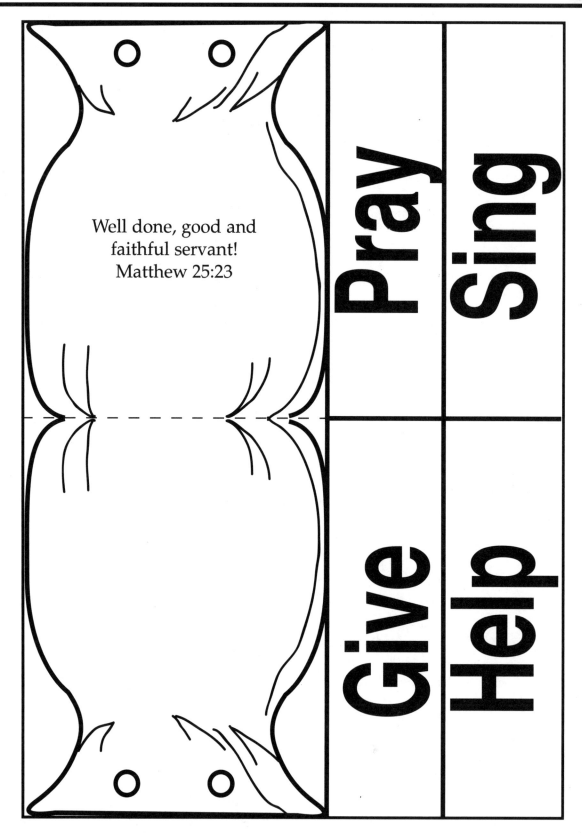

Well done, good and faithful servant!
Matthew 25:23

Pray

Sing

Give

Help

The Good Samaritan
Luke 10:30-37

MEMORY VERSE

Love…God with all your heart…Love your neighbor as yourself.
~ Luke 10:27

WHAT YOU NEED

- page 36, duplicated
- crayons
- safety scissors
- hole punch
- yarn
- tape

BEFORE CLASS

Duplicate a pattern page for each child. For younger children, cut out the four rectangles. Poke a hole in each large dot. Cut a one-yard length of yarn for each child. Make a sample craft to show the children.

WHAT TO DO

1. Introduce the lesson by telling the story of the Good Samaritan from Luke 10:30-37. Say, **Jesus wants us to remember to be kind to others. The good neighbor stopped to help the hurt man. We can all help others and be good neighbors.**
2. Show the children the sample craft.
3. Distribute a pattern page to each child.
4. Say the memory verse.
5. Have the children cut out the four rectangles. Help the children poke two holes at the top of each and lay them in order.
6. Help the students thread the yarn through the holes, as shown.
7. Tape the yarn in one spot on the back of each rectangle.
8. Have the children color the rectangles. Read the phrases aloud. Have them point to Jesus and say, "Love God with all your heart." Have them point to the Samaritan and say, "Love your neighbor as yourself."

EXTRA TIME

Cut out two or more hearts from red or pink construction paper. Poke a hole in the sides of each heart. Using four or five feet of yarn, show how to string the hearts and rectangles onto the yarn.

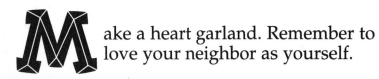 ake a heart garland. Remember to love your neighbor as yourself.

The Rich Fool
Luke 12:16-21

MEMORY VERSE

Share with God's people who are in need.
~ Romans 12:13

WHAT YOU NEED

- page 38, duplicated
- crayons
- tape
- red construction paper
- glue (optional)

BEFORE CLASS

Duplicate a pattern page for each child. Cut the four slits in the barn picture. Cut four strips that are 1" wide and 6" long from red construction paper for each child. Make a sample craft to show the children.

WHAT TO DO

1. Introduce the lesson by telling the story from Luke 12:16-21. Say, **God wasn't happy with the man who had a lot but wouldn't share. God wants us to share with others.**
2. Show the children the sample craft.
3. Distribute a pattern page to each child.
4. Say the memory verse.
5. Have the children weave the four strips through the slits, with most of the red showing on the outside of the picture. Option: For younger preschoolers, you may choose to have them glue the strips to the picture instead of making slits in the page.
6. Have the children color the page as time allows. Discuss things we can share with others. Suggest: food, money, clothes, toys, time to help others, etc.

EXTRA TIME

Make banks for the children to take home. Give each child a copy of the page and a gallon milk jug. Spread glue on the back of the picture and center the picture on the milk jug, opposite the handle. Put the lids on the jugs. Say, **We made banks so we can save our money and share with others.**

ake a barn weaving. Remember
that God wants us to share with
him and with others.

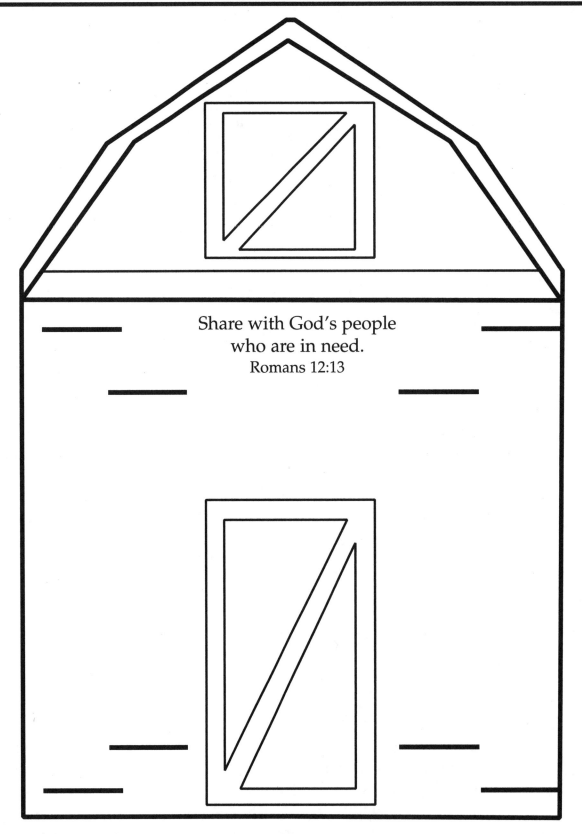

Share with God's people
who are in need.
Romans 12:13

The Lost Coin
Luke 15:8-10

MEMORY VERSE

There is rejoicing...over one sinner who repents.
~ Luke 15:10

WHAT YOU NEED

- page 40, duplicated
- crayons
- tape
- paper towel tubes

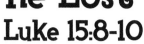

BEFORE CLASS

Duplicate a pattern page for each child. Make a sample craft to show the children.

WHAT TO DO

1. Introduce the lesson by telling the story from Luke 15:8-10. Say, **We are happy when we find something special we have lost. We are special to God. He is happy when we become His children and are no longer lost.**
2. Show the children the sample craft.
3. Distribute a pattern page to each child.
4. Say the memory verse.
5. Have the children color the page.
6. Show how to roll the page around a paper towel tube, overlapping the blank part. Tape on the seam. Let the children practice rejoicing in song using their praise horns.

EXTRA TIME

Add some paper streamers by taping 1" x 5" strips to the bottom end of the horn.

ake a praise horn to rejoice in finding a lost coin. God rejoices in finding a lost person.

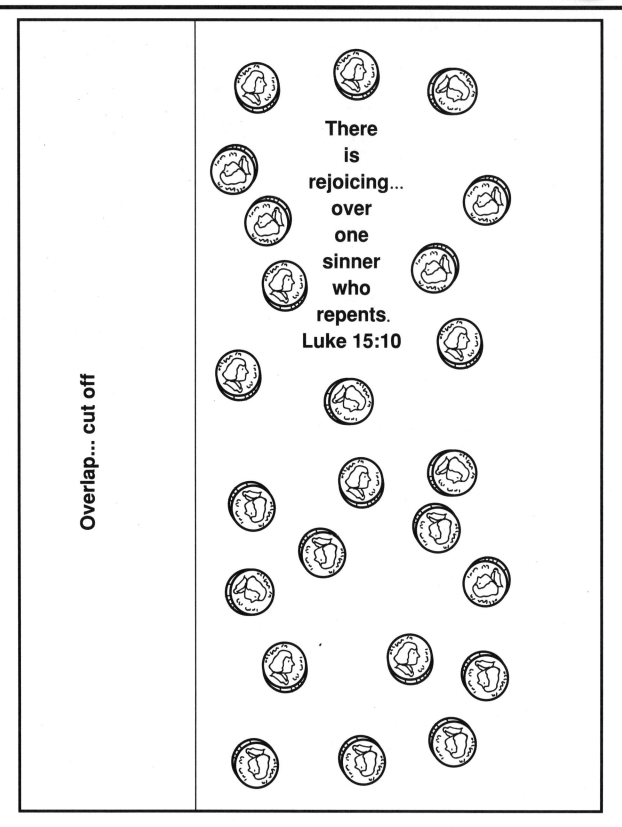

There is rejoicing... over one sinner who repents. Luke 15:10

Overlap... cut off

The Lost Son
Luke 15:11-32

MEMORY VERSE

This son...was lost and is found.
~ Luke 15:24

WHAT YOU NEED

- page 42, duplicated
- crayons
- safety scissors

BEFORE CLASS

Duplicate a pattern page for each child. For younger preschoolers, cut the page on the solid line. Make a sample craft to show the children.

WHAT TO DO

1. Introduce the lesson by telling the story from Luke 15:11-32. Say, **Just like the son who left home and came back, God is happy when each of us becomes His child. God wants us to live for Him.**
2. Show the children the sample craft.
3. Distribute a pattern page to each child.
4. Say the memory verse.
5. Have the children cut the page on the solid line.
6. Help them fold the two figures on the fold line.
7. Have the children color the figures as time allows. Have the children use their figures to retell the story. Encourage the children to rejoice when the lost son is found.

EXTRA TIME

Play "Lost and Found." Use the son figure from the pattern page. Show the children the son. Then have the children close their eyes as you partially hide the son. Have the children stay seated as they look for the lost son. Play the game several times to give more children a chance to be the "finder."

ake a stand-up scene to tell the story of the son who ran away, but returned.

This son…was lost and is found.
Luke 15:24

42

The Growing Seed
Mark 4:26-29

MEMORY VERSE

All by itself the soil produces grain.
~ Mark 4:28

WHAT YOU NEED

- page 44, duplicated
- crayons
- safety scissors
- tape
- juice can
- dirt and seeds (optional)

BEFORE CLASS

Duplicate a pattern page for each child. For younger children, cut out the strip. Make a sample craft to show the children.

WHAT TO DO

1. Introduce the lesson by telling the parable from Mark 4:26-29. Say, **Jesus says that when we plant a seed it grows even when we aren't watching it. That's how God's Kingdom is. Good things happen even when we aren't watching.**
2. Show the children the sample craft.
3. Distribute a pattern page to each child.
4. Say the memory verse.
5. Help the children cut out the strip.
6. Have them color the strip as time allows.
7. Help the children tape the strip around the juice can. Say, **Our planter reminds us of the story Jesus told. We can remember that good things happen in God's Kingdom, even when we don't expect it.**

EXTRA TIME

Show the children how to cut out the three insects on the page. Allow them to glue the insects to the planter. Help the student fill the containers with dirt, then show how to plant some seeds.

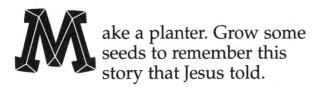 ake a planter. Grow some seeds to remember this story that Jesus told.

All by itself the soil produces grain.
Mark 4:28

The Two Debtors
Luke 4:41-43

MEMORY VERSE

Praise the Lord...who forgives all your sins.
~ Psalm 103:2-3

Praise the Lord...
who forgives
all your sins.

Psalm 103:2-3

WHAT YOU NEED

- page 46, duplicated
- heavy white paper or card stock
- crayons
- safety scissors
- tape

BEFORE CLASS

Duplicate a pattern page on heavy white paper or card stock for each child. For younger preschoolers, cut out the bank. Make a sample craft to show the children.

WHAT TO DO

1. Introduce the lesson by telling the story from Luke 7:41-43. Say, **One man begged to be forgiven. But he wouldn't forgive another person who owed him money. Jesus says we should always forgive others.**
2. Show the children the sample craft.
3. Distribute a pattern page to each child.
4. Say the memory verse.
5. Have the children cut out the bank. Help them cut the slit in the top.
6. Allow the children to color the bank if time permits.
7. Show how to fold the bank on the dashed lines and tape it at the seams. Discuss forgiveness. Ask the children to tell about times they have forgiven someone.

EXTRA TIME

Allow the children to make two banks, one for themselves and one for a friend. Discuss love and forgiveness while the children work.

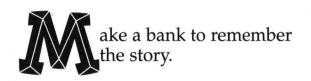 ake a bank to remember
the story.

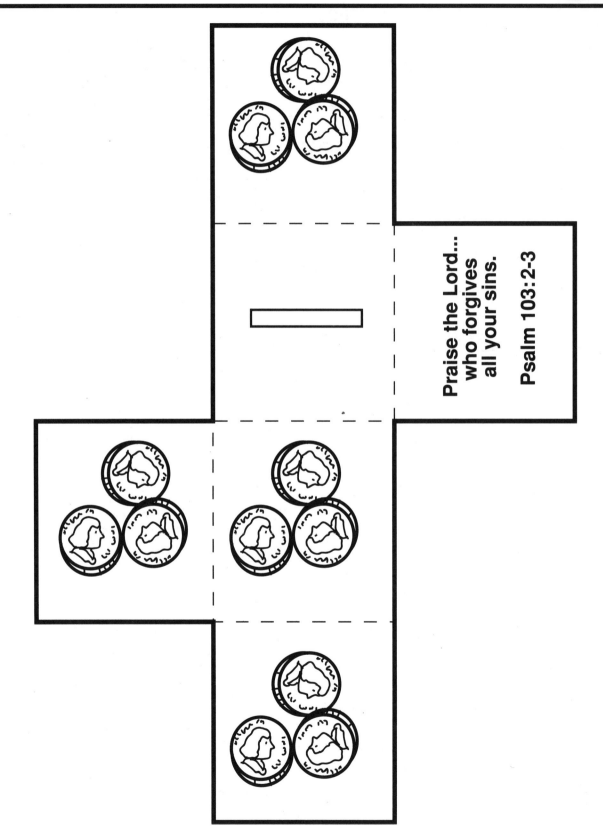

Praise the Lord...
who forgives
all your sins.

Psalm 103:2-3

The Pharisee and Tax Collector
Luke 18:9-14

MEMORY VERSE

Be completely humble.
~ Ephesians 4:2

> But the tax collector cried, "God, I am a sinner!"

WHAT YOU NEED

- page 48, duplicated
- crayons
- tape

BEFORE CLASS

Duplicate a pattern page for each child. Make a sample craft to show the children.

WHAT TO DO

1. Introduce the lesson by telling the story from Luke 18:9-14. Say, **Jesus wants us to be humble, not proud. We should not brag about how wonderful we are. We should ask God to forgive our sins and help us to be better.**
2. Show the children the sample craft.
3. Distribute a pattern page to each child.
4. Say the memory verse.
5. Have the children fold the page in half. Help the children tape the top and side of the puppet.
6. While the children color the puppet, retell the Bible story. Discuss pride and humility. Say, **Jesus doesn't want us to have so much pride that we think we are better than others.**

EXTRA TIME

Allow time for the children to practice retelling the story in their own words. Prepare the children to be able to use their puppet to tell the story at home.

ake a double-sided puppet to tell the Bible story. Jesus tells us to be humble when we pray, not proud.

But the tax collector cried, "God, I am a sinner!"

The Pharisee stood up and prayed about himself.

Jesus Taught People About God

Matthew 9:18-26

MEMORY VERSE

Jesus began to teach by the lake.
~ Mark 4:1

WHAT YOU NEED

- page 50, duplicated
- heavy white paper or card stock
- crayons
- safety scissors
- tape

BEFORE CLASS

Duplicate a pattern page onto heavy white paper or card stock. For younger children, cut out the corner squares. Make a sample craft to show the children.

WHAT TO DO

1. Introduce the lesson by telling about Jesus teaching the people from Mark 4:1. Say, **Wherever Jesus went, many people gathered. People loved to listen to Jesus teach them about God. We gather at our churches to learn about God, too.** You may also want to use another example of Jesus teaching, such as Matthew chapters 5-7.
2. Show the children the sample craft.
3. Distribute a pattern page to each child.
4. Say the memory verse.
5. Have the children cut off the corner squares.
6. While the children color the picture of Jesus teaching the crowd, talk about the scene.
7. Help the children fold and tape the corners to form a frame. Ask the children to tell about a favorite Bible story they have learned at church.

EXTRA TIME

Pencil in letters to spell JESUS, above the scene. Help the children spread glue on the letters and sprinkle them with glitter.

ake a framed picture that shows
Jesus teaching the people.

Jesus began to teach by the lake.
Mark 4:1

Jesus Turns Water into Wine
John 2:1-11

MEMORY VERSE

His disciples put their faith in him.
~ John 2:11

His disciples put their faith in him.
John 2:11

WHAT YOU NEED

- page 52, duplicated
- watercolor or tempera paint
- paint brushes or cotton swabs
- paint smocks

BEFORE CLASS

Duplicate a pattern page for each child. Make a sample craft to show the children.

WHAT TO DO

1. Introduce the lesson by telling about the miracle from John 2:1-11. Say, **Jesus did a miracle to help His friends and to show He was God's Son. When Jesus' friends saw the wonderful things He could do, they put their faith in Him.**
2. Show the children the sample craft.
3. Distribute a pattern page to each child.
4. Say the memory verse.
5. Have the children put on paint smocks.
6. While the children paint the pictures, retell the story. Discuss faith in Jesus. Say, **We believe in Jesus because we know He is God's Son.**

EXTRA TIME

Bring a clear container of water. As you retell the Bible story, add a packet of red drink mix and shake or stir. Say, **Jesus turned the water into wine, but He did it without adding anything. Only Jesus can do miracles. He did this miracle to help His friends. Jesus always helps His friends.** Then ask, **Who here is a friend of Jesus?**

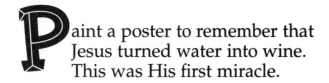

aint a poster to remember that Jesus turned water into wine. This was His first miracle.

His disciples put their faith in him.
John 2:11

The Large Catch of Fish
Luke 5:1-11

MEMORY VERSE

They...filled both boats so full that they began to sink.
~ Luke 5:7

WHAT YOU NEED

- page 54, duplicated
- crayons

BEFORE CLASS

Duplicate a pattern page for each child.

WHAT TO DO

1. Introduce the lesson by telling the story from Luke 5:1-11. Say, **The men had fished all night, but they didn't catch any fish. Then Jesus did a miracle and made the nets fill with fish. The fishermen were surprised and believed in Jesus.**
2. Distribute a pattern page to each child.
3. Say the memory verse.
4. Have the children circle the one fish in each row that is different. Say, **Jesus helped His friends catch many fish. Let's find some fish that are different than the others.**

EXTRA TIME

Have the children turn the page over and draw some fish. Provide a piece of netting or onion bag for the children to glue over their fish.

Do a fun puzzle to remember
that Jesus helped His friends
catch many fish.

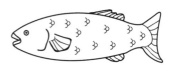  

 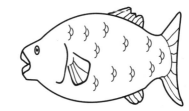 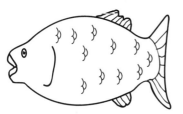

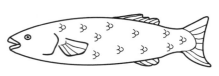 

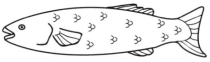

Jesus Calms the Storm
Mark 4:35-41

MEMORY VERSE

Even the wind and the waves obey him!
~ Mark 4:41

WHAT YOU NEED

- page 56, duplicated
- crayons
- tape

BEFORE CLASS

Duplicate a pattern page for each child. Make a sample craft to show the children.

WHAT TO DO

1. Introduce the lesson by telling the story from Mark 4:35-41. Say, **Jesus performed a miracle when He stopped the wind and waves. Only God's Son could stop the storm.**
2. Show the children the sample craft.
3. Distribute a pattern page to each child.
4. Say the memory verse.
5. Help the children fold the page on the dashed lines.
6. Show the children how to fold the bottom portion of the scene up and down to tell the story.
7. Have the children color the scene as time allows. Discuss how the wind blows and the rain comes down during a storm. Say, **Jesus' friends were amazed when the wind and rain obeyed Jesus and stopped suddenly.**

EXTRA TIME

Turn the activity into a crayon resist. Have the children color the boat scene. Then provide thinned blue paint or watercolors, along with brushes or bits of sponge. Have the children cover the page with blue paint (you might want the children to put on paint smocks first). The wax in the crayon will resist the paint.

ake a folding picture to help tell the story. Jesus performed a miracle when He stopped the wind and the waves.

Even the wind and the waves obey him!

Mark 4:41

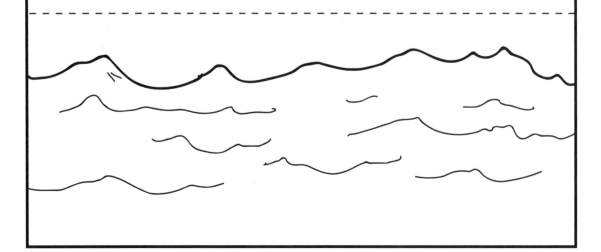

Jesus Feeds 5,000
John 6:5-15

MEMORY VERSE

Jesus...gave thanks.
~ John 6:11

WHAT YOU NEED

- page 58, duplicated
- crayons
- construction paper
- tape or glue

BEFORE CLASS

Duplicate a pattern page for each child. Cut a 2" x 8" strip of construction paper for each child. Make a sample craft to show the children.

WHAT TO DO

1. Introduce the lesson by telling the story from John 6:5-15. Say, **Jesus wanted to help all the hungry people. Jesus wants to help us, too.**
2. Show the children the sample craft.
3. Distribute a pattern page to each child.
4. Say the memory verse.
5. While the children color the lunch, retell the story.
6. Help the children tape or glue a construction paper handle to the page to form a basket. Have the children help you count the five loaves of bread and two fish. Stress that Jesus did a miracle to make enough food to feed all these people and still have some leftover.

EXTRA TIME

Provide fish-shaped crackers and round crackers for the children to glue inside the shapes on the page.

ake a picnic lunch to remember that
Jesus did this miracle. He fed over
5,000 people with a very small lunch.

Jesus…gave thanks.
~ John 6:11

Jesus Heals a Nobleman's Son
John 4:46-54

MEMORY VERSE

Jesus had said to him, "Your son will live."
~ John 4:53

WHAT YOU NEED

- page 60, duplicated
- crayons
- safety scissors
- tape

BEFORE CLASS

Duplicate a pattern page for each child. For younger children, cut the page apart on the solid line. Make a sample craft to show the children.

WHAT TO DO

1. Introduce the lesson by telling the story from John 4:46-54. Say, **Jesus showed people how much He loved them by healing them. Jesus loves us very much.**
2. Show the children the sample craft.
3. Distribute a pattern page to each child.
4. Say the memory verse.
5. Have the children cut the page on the solid line.
6. Help the children fold the two strips in half and tape the sides.
7. Have the children color their puppets as time allows. Talk about how thankful each child's parents would be if they were sick and then were made well.

EXTRA TIME

Have the children use their puppets to act out the story.

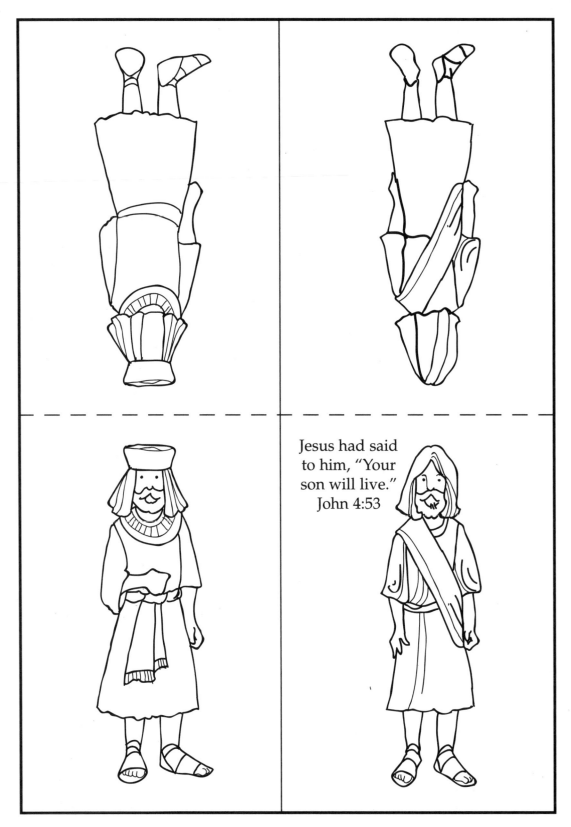

Jesus had said to him, "Your son will live." John 4:53

Jesus Heals Peter's Mother-in-law
Matthew 8:14-15

MEMORY VERSE
He touched her hand and the fever left her. ~ Matthew 8:15

WHAT YOU NEED

- page 62, duplicated
- heavy white paper or card stock
- crayons
- safety scissors

BEFORE CLASS

Duplicate a pattern page on heavy white paper or card stock for each child. Make a sample craft to show the children.

WHAT TO DO

1. Introduce the lesson by telling the story from Matthew 8:14-15. Say, **Jesus didn't have to use medicine or doctor's tools to make the woman well. He just touched her hand and His power made her well. Jesus is truly God's Son.**
2. Show the children the sample craft.
3. Distribute a pattern page to each child.
4. Say the memory verse.
5. While the children color the page, retell the story.
6. Have the children cut the page on the solid lines. Older children may cut the page into more pieces.
7. Show how to manipulate the puzzle pieces. Pray with the children and thank God for the miraculous healing of Peter's mother-in-law. Then mention the good things God does daily in the children's lives.

EXTRA TIME

Help the children cover the page with clear, adhesive-backed plastic before cutting the puzzle into pieces.

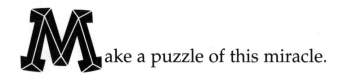 ake a puzzle of this miracle.

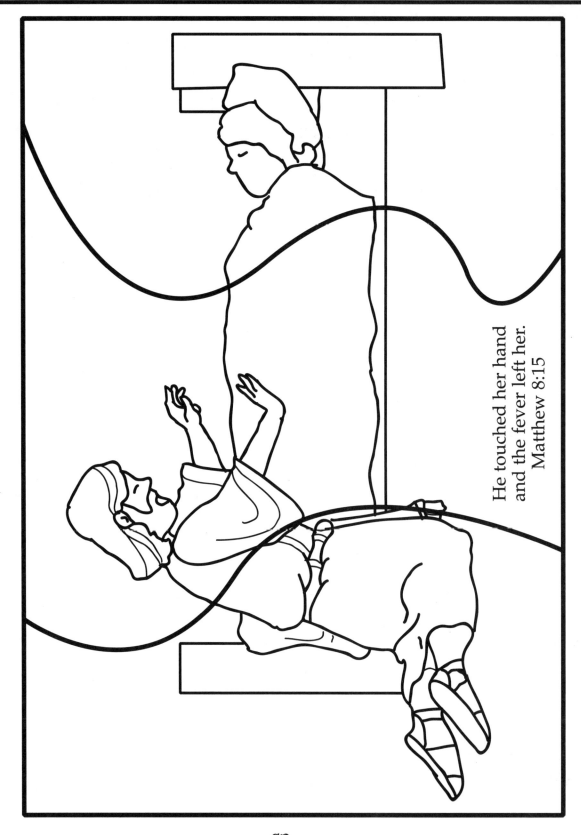

He touched her hand and the fever left her.
Matthew 8:15

Jesus Heals a Leper
Mark 1:40-45

MEMORY VERSE

"If you are willing, you can make me clean [well]."
~ Mark 1:40

WHAT YOU NEED

- page 64, duplicated
- crayons
- safety scissors
- tape

BEFORE CLASS

Duplicate a pattern page for each child. For younger children, cut the page apart on the solid line. Make a sample craft to show the children.

WHAT TO DO

1. Introduce the lesson by telling the story from Mark 1:40-45. Say, **The man believed Jesus could help him. Jesus wants us to believe in Him.**
2. Show the children the sample craft.
3. Distribute a pattern page to each child.
4. Say the memory verse.
5. Have the children cut on the solid line to separate the strip from the page. Tape the strip to the top of the page, where indicated.
6. Show the children how to flip the picture back and forth to tell the story.
7. Have the children color the pictures as time allows. Say, **Jesus is happy when we believe in Him. He wants to be our friend and our Lord.**

EXTRA TIME

Instead of coloring, have the children dab paint onto the pictures using a small bit of sponge and water colors or tempera paint (you might want to help them into paint smocks first).

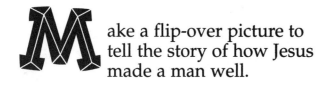

ake a flip-over picture to tell the story of how Jesus made a man well.

"If you are willing, you can make me clean [well]."
Mark 1:40

Friends Know Jesus Heals
Luke 5:17-26

MEMORY VERSE

He stood up... and went home praising God.
~ Luke 5:25

He stood up... and went home praising God.
Luke 5:25

WHAT YOU NEED

- page 66, duplicated
- crayons
- safety scissors
- tape
- yarn

BEFORE CLASS

Duplicate pattern page for each child. For younger children, cut the page on the solid lines. Cut two 6-inch lengths of yarn for each child. Make a sample craft to show the children.

WHAT TO DO

1. Introduce the lesson by telling the story from Luke 5:17-26. Say, **Some friends wanted Jesus to heal a crippled man. They lowered him into the crowded house through the roof. Jesus was glad the friends knew He could heal the crippled man.**
2. Show the children the sample craft.
3. Distribute a pattern page to each child.
4. Say the memory verse.
5. Have the children cut the page on the solid lines.
6. Help children fold the figure on the broken lines, then tape the yarn to each end of the figure. Tape the other ends of the yarn to the top of the scene.
7. Have the children color the scene as time allows.
8. Show how to move the figure to tell the story. Talk about how the children could help a sick friend by praying for him or her.

EXTRA TIME

Poke two holes at the top of the page, and thread two 10-inch lengths of yarn through the holes. Tie together. At the other end of the yarn lengths, tape the figure of the man on the mat. Show the children how to pull the yarn at the back of the picture to raise and lower the mat.

esus healed a man who was lowered through the roof, because the house was so crowded. Make a picture to remember the story.

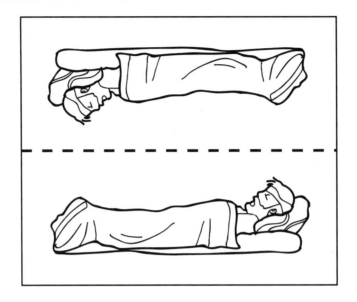

He stood up... and went home praising God.
Luke 5:25

Jesus Walks on Water
Matthew 14:22-33

Matthew
14:22-33

WHAT YOU NEED

- page 68, duplicated
- crayons

BEFORE CLASS

Duplicate a pattern page for each child.

WHAT TO DO

1. Introduce the lesson by telling the story of Jesus walking on the water, from Matthew 14:22-33. Say, **Jesus' friends were afraid at first. They didn't think anyone could walk on water. Jesus proved He can do special things because He is God's Son.**
2. Distribute a pattern page to each child.
3. Say the memory verse.
4. Have the children shade in the shapes with a dot. Ask, **Who is walking on the water?**
5. Have the children color the picture as time allows. Remind the children that Jesus could do miracles like walking on water because He is God's Son.

EXTRA TIME

Teach this little song to your students to the tune of "The Bear Went Over the Mountain":

Jesus walked on the water.
Jesus walked on the water.
Jesus walked on the water.
Because He is God's Son.

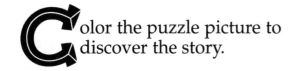 olor the puzzle picture to
discover the story.

Matthew
14:22-33

The Tax Money
Matthew 17:24-27

MEMORY VERSE

Open its mouth and you will find a...coin.
~ Matthew 17:27

WHAT YOU NEED

- page 70, duplicated
- crayons
- safety scissors
- glue

BEFORE CLASS

Duplicate a pattern page for each child. For younger children, cut the coin and verse pieces. Make a sample craft to show the children.

WHAT TO DO

1. Introduce the lesson by telling the story from Matthew 17:24-27. Ask, **Where did Jesus' helpers find the coin to pay the tax? How did the coin get in the fish's mouth? Yes, it was a miracle. Jesus did miracles to show He is God's Son.**
2. Show the children the sample craft.
3. Distribute a pattern page to each child.
4. Say the memory verse.
5. Have the children cut the coin and verse shapes from the page.
6. Have the children fold the fish in half.
7. Help the children glue the coin and verse figures inside the fish.
8. Have the children color the fish as time allows. Say, **Jesus caused a coin to be in the fish's mouth. He told Peter to catch a fish and there would be a coin inside.**

EXTRA TIME

Provide sticker dots with which the children may decorate the fish.

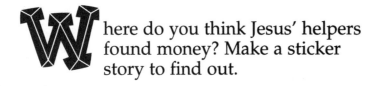 **W**here do you think Jesus' helpers found money? Make a sticker story to find out.

Open its mouth and you will find a…coin.
Matthew 17:27

Jesus Helps Disciples Catch Fish
John 21:1-14

It was full of large fish,...but the net was not torn.
John 21:11

MEMORY VERSE

It was full of large fish,...but the net was not torn.
~ John 21:11

WHAT YOU NEED

- page 72, duplicated
- crayons

BEFORE CLASS

Duplicate a pattern page for
each child. Make a sample craft to show the children. Be sure to have
plenty of brown and gray crayons on hand.

WHAT TO DO

1. Introduce the lesson by telling the story found in John 21:1-14. Say,
   **Not only did Jesus cause the net to be filled with fish, He also
   caused the net not to tear. Jesus thinks of everything!**
2. Show the children the sample craft.
3. Distribute a pattern page to each child.
4. Say the memory verse.
5. Tell the children to color all parts of the picture that have a "1"
   brown, and all the parts that have a "2" gray. Retell the story. Stress
   that this miracle happened after Jesus had died and risen again.

EXTRA TIME

Play the Fish Net Game. Arrange the children in a circle and have them
hold hands. Say the verse below while the children step back farther and
farther as they continue to hold hands.
The men didn't catch any fish.
Then Jesus said, "Try again."
The net got fuller and fuller of fish.
Then fuller and fuller and fuller.
But it still didn't break.

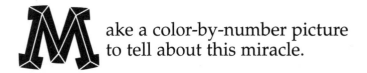 ake a color-by-number picture
to tell about this miracle.

It was full of large fish,...but the net was not torn.
John 21:11

72

Jesus Helps a Man Walk
John 5:1-15

MEMORY VERSE

At once the man was cured.
~ John 5:9

At once the man was cured.
John 5:9

WHAT YOU NEED

- page 74, duplicated
- crayons

BEFORE CLASS

Duplicate a pattern page for each child. Make a sample craft to show the children.

WHAT TO DO

1. Introduce the lesson by telling the story from John 5:5-15. Say, **When Jesus made the man well, he didn't say, "I am Jesus." He just made the man well because He cared. Later, Jesus told the man to stop sinning. Then the man knew it was Jesus who made him well. Jesus cares about each of us.**
2. Show the children the sample craft.
3. Distribute a pattern page to each child.
4. Say the memory verse.
5. Have the children color the picture.
6. Show how to fold the picture on the dashed line.
7. Show how to hide the bottom portion and then reveal it to tell the story. Retell the story, stressing that Jesus cared about the man who couldn't walk, and He cares about us.

EXTRA TIME

Have the children glue small pieces of construction paper to the well and to the rock surface of the ground.

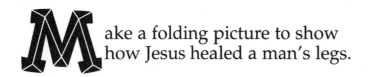 ake a folding picture to show
how Jesus healed a man's legs.

At once the man was cured.
John 5:9

Jesus Heals a Man's Hand
Mark 3:1-6

MEMORY VERSE

His hand was completely restored.
~ Mark 3:5

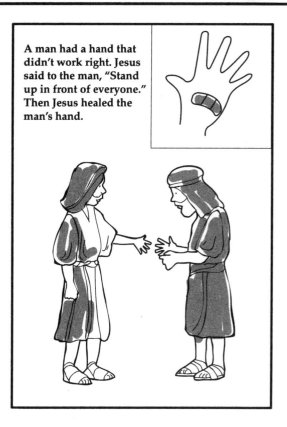

A man had a hand that didn't work right. Jesus said to the man, "Stand up in front of everyone." Then Jesus healed the man's hand.

WHAT YOU NEED

- page 76, duplicated
- crayons
- adhesive bandages

BEFORE CLASS

Duplicate a pattern page for each child. Make a sample craft to show the children.

WHAT TO DO

1. Introduce the lesson by telling the story in Mark 3:1-6. Say, **Even though some of the people were trying to find Jesus doing something wrong, Jesus healed the man's hand. It was on a day when no one was supposed to work. Jesus is Lord over sickness every day of the week. Jesus is Lord of all.**
2. Show the children the sample craft.
3. Distribute a pattern page to each child.
4. Say the memory verse.
5. Have the children place a bandage over the hand.
6. Allow the children to color the picture as time allows. Repeat, **Jesus is Lord of all.**

EXTRA TIME

Trace the children's hands on the back of their pictures. Allow them to place bandage strips on the hands, or draw bandages.

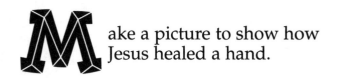

A man had a hand that didn't work right. Jesus said to the man, "Stand up in front of everyone." Then Jesus healed the man's hand.

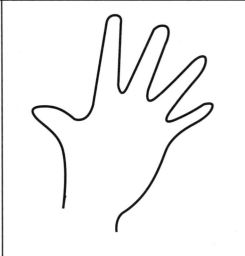

Mark 3:1-6

Jesus Heals a Centurion Servant

Luke 7:1-10

MEMORY VERSE

I have not found such great faith.
~ Luke 7:9

WHAT YOU NEED

- page 78, duplicated
- crayons
- safety scissors
- tape
- yarn

BEFORE CLASS

Duplicate a pattern page. For younger children, cut the page in half on the solid line. Cut two lengths of yarn for each child, around two feet long each. Make a sample craft to show the children.

WHAT TO DO

1. Introduce the lesson by telling the story found in Luke 7:1-10. Say, **Jesus was happy to find someone who had such faith. Jesus is happy when we have faith and trust in Him.**
2. Show the children the sample craft.
3. Distribute a pattern page to each child.
4. Say the memory verse.
5. Have the children cut on the solid line to separate the two pendants.
6. Help the children fold the pendants on the dashed lines.
7. Place a length of yarn on the inside of the pendant, at the folded edge. Tape in one place to hold. Tie the yarn to form a neck chain.
8. Have the children color the pendants as time allows.
9. Encourage the children to wear one pendant and give the other to a friend. Have the children wave one pendant while you lead them in a praise song.

EXTRA TIME

Explain what faith is. Have the children trace the letters with a crayon. Provide "praying hands" stickers for the children to put on their pendant. Tell the children, **We show faith in Jesus by praying and trusting.**

Make pendants to tell that the Centurion had faith in Jesus. Wear one pendant and give the other to a friend.

I have not found
such great faith.

Luke 7:9

I have not found
such great faith.

Luke 7:9

FAITH

FAITH

Jesus Helps a Man to See & Hear
Matthew 12:22

MEMORY VERSE

Jesus healed him so he could talk and see.
~ Matthew 12:22

WHAT YOU NEED

- page 80, duplicated
- crayons
- safety scissors
- tape

BEFORE CLASS

Duplicate a pattern page for each child. For younger children, cut out the two pieces. Cut out the square in the man's head. Make a sample craft to show the children.

WHAT TO DO

1. Introduce the lesson by telling the story found in Matthew 12:22. Say, **The man couldn't see or talk. Then Jesus made him well. The man and all the people saw the wonderful things God's Son could do. We can learn from our Bibles all the wonderful things Jesus did.**
2. Show the sample craft to the children.
3. Distribute a pattern page to each child.
4. Say the memory verse.
5. Have the children cut out the two pieces. Help the children cut out the square from the man's head.
6. Have the children fold the large piece in half on the dashed lines. Tape it at the open side.
7. Help the children insert the small strip inside the folded piece. Show how to move the strip to make the man's eyes and mouth open and close.
8. Have the children color the figure as time allows. Have the children help you retell the story in their own words, using the moving picture.

EXTRA TIME

Play a game in which you have the children try to put together a puzzle or color a picture with their eyes closed. Have them try to communicate with each other without speaking.

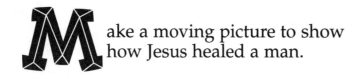 **M**ake a moving picture to show how Jesus healed a man.

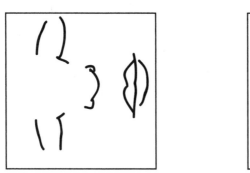

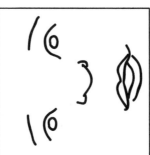

Jesus healed him so he could talk and see. Matthew 12:22

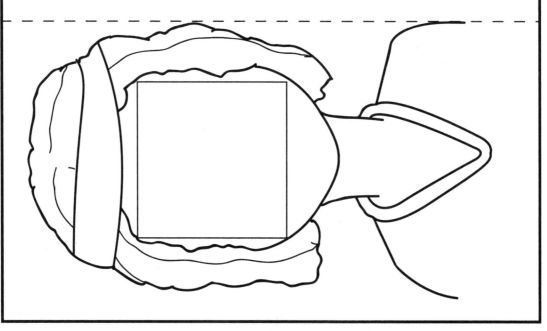

Jesus Heals a Little Girl
Matthew 9:18-26

MEMORY VERSE

He ... took the girl by the hand, and she got up.
~ Matthew 9:25

WHAT YOU NEED

- page 82, duplicated
- crayons
- safety scissors
- tape

BEFORE CLASS

Duplicate a pattern page for each child. For younger children, cut out the badge. Make a sample craft to show the children.

WHAT TO DO

1. Introduce the lesson by telling the story from Matthew 9:18-26. Say, **The little girl's father had faith that Jesus could make the girl alive again. Jesus loves when we have faith in Him.**
2. Show the children the sample craft.
3. Distribute a pattern page to each child.
4. Say the memory verse.
5. Have the children cut out the badge and fold it on the dashed line. Tape the edge in at least one spot.
6. Have the children color the badge.
7. Fasten the badge to the children's clothing with a loop of tape. Say, Jesus loves each of us. He wants to help us.

EXTRA TIME

Cut the badge along the dashed line to make two badges. Have the children color the illustrated badge, and decorate the blank one as they wish.

ake a badge to show that Jesus loves you, just as He loved the little girl.

He...took the girl by the hand, and she got up. Matthew 9:25

A Woman Touches Jesus' Clothing
Mark 5:25-34

MEMORY VERSE

Your faith has healed you.
~ Mark 5:34

WHAT YOU NEED

- page 84, duplicated
- crayons

BEFORE CLASS

Duplicate a pattern page for each child. Make a sample craft to show the children.

WHAT TO DO

1. Introduce the lesson by telling the story from Mark 5:25-34. Say, **The woman touched Jesus' clothing and was healed. Jesus said she had great faith.**
2. Show the children the sample craft.
3. Distribute a pattern page to each child.
4. Say the memory verse.
5. Have the children fold the page into a booklet.
6. Tell the children to connect the dots to complete each picture. Have the children color the pictures as time allows. Have the children retell the story, using their booklets. Stress that Jesus was happy the woman had great faith.

EXTRA TIME

Play the Faith Game. Put a few pieces of candy in each of six paper bags. Tape the tops closed. Pass three bags around and let the children shake them. Ask, **Do you have faith that there is something in these bags?** Repeat with the other three bags. Ask again, **Do you have faith that there is something in these bags?** Discuss that many people saw Jesus do miracles and believed. Others only heard about Jesus, yet they believed and had faith, too.

esus told the woman her faith had healed her. Follow the dots in the booklet to complete pictures from the story.

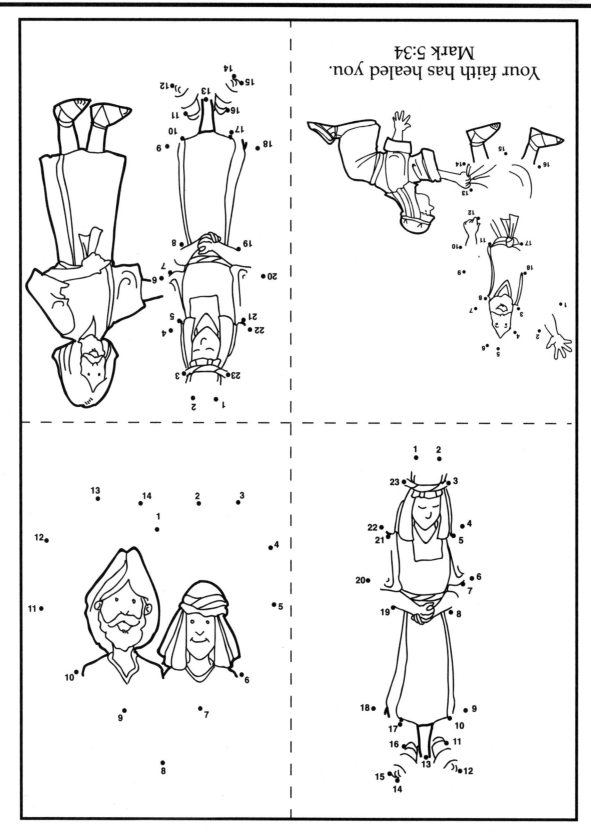

84

Jesus Heals Ten Lepers
Luke 17:11-19

MEMORY VERSE

One…came back, praising God.
~ Luke 17:15

WHAT YOU NEED

- page 86, duplicated
- crayons
- safety scissors
- tape
- plastic drinking straws or craft sticks, two per child

BEFORE CLASS

Duplicate a pattern page for each child. For younger children, cut on the bold line to form two puppets. Make a sample craft to show the children.

WHAT TO DO

1. Introduce the lesson by telling the story from Luke 17:11-19. Say, **Jesus healed 10 men. But only one praised God and thanked Jesus. Jesus wants us to praise God and be thankful.**
2. Show the children the sample craft.
3. Distribute a pattern page to each child.
4. Say the memory verse.
5. Have the children cut apart the puppets on the solid line.
6. Show how to fold the two strips in half.
7. Help the children tape a craft stick or straw to the inside of each puppet strip, and tape the sides of each puppet.
8. Have the children color the puppets as time allows. Lead the children in prayer to thank and praise God. Suggest: for Sunday school, for families, for making someone well, etc.

EXTRA TIME

Make modern-day puppets. Have the children cut out pictures of people from magazines. Glue one picture to a square of construction paper, then tape a straw or craft stick to the back. Encourage the children to have their puppets thank God for something.

esus healed 10 men from leprosy. Do you know how many returned to thank Jesus? Make some puppets to tell the story.

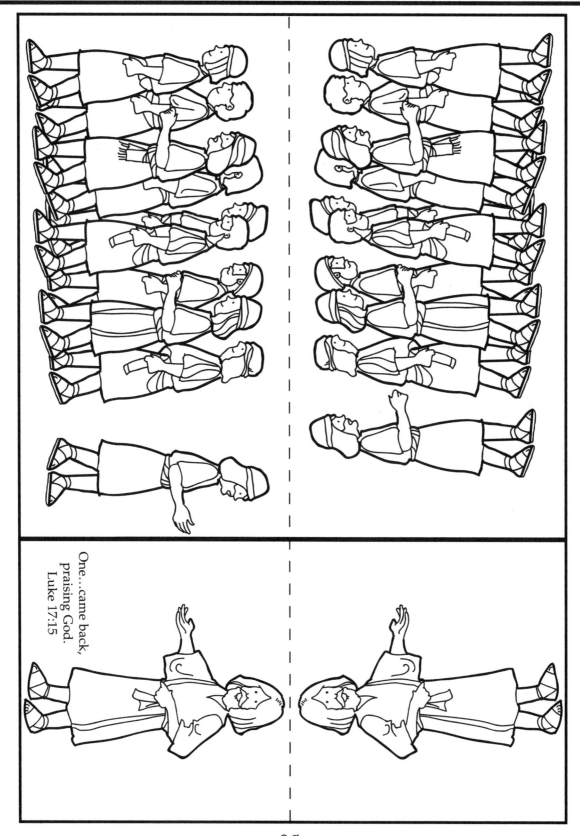

One...came back, praising God.
Luke 17:15

Jesus Heals Blind Bartimaeus
Mark 10:46-52

MEMORY VERSE

He received his sight and followed Jesus.
~ Mark 10:52

WHAT YOU NEED

- page 88, duplicated
- heavy white paper or card stock
- crayons
- safety scissors

BEFORE CLASS

Duplicate a pattern page onto heavy white paper or card stock for each child. For younger children, cut out the glasses. Make a sample craft to show the children.

WHAT TO DO

1. Introduce the lesson by telling the story from Mark 10:46-52. Say, **Bartimaeus didn't just thank Jesus. He began to follow as Jesus taught and healed people. Jesus wants us to follow Him as well as thank Him.**
2. Show the children the sample craft.
3. Distribute a pattern page to each child.
4. Say the memory verse.
5. Have the children cut out the glasses.
6. Have the children color the glasses as time allows.
7. Encourage the children to put on the glasses and try to see. Have the children take off their glasses and thank God that they can see.

EXTRA TIME

Provide two pattern sheets for each child. Help the children cut out the center "lenses" of one pair of glasses. Then the children can play-act the story, using the "blind" glasses and the "seeing" glasses.

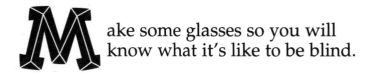 ake some glasses so you will
know what it's like to be blind.

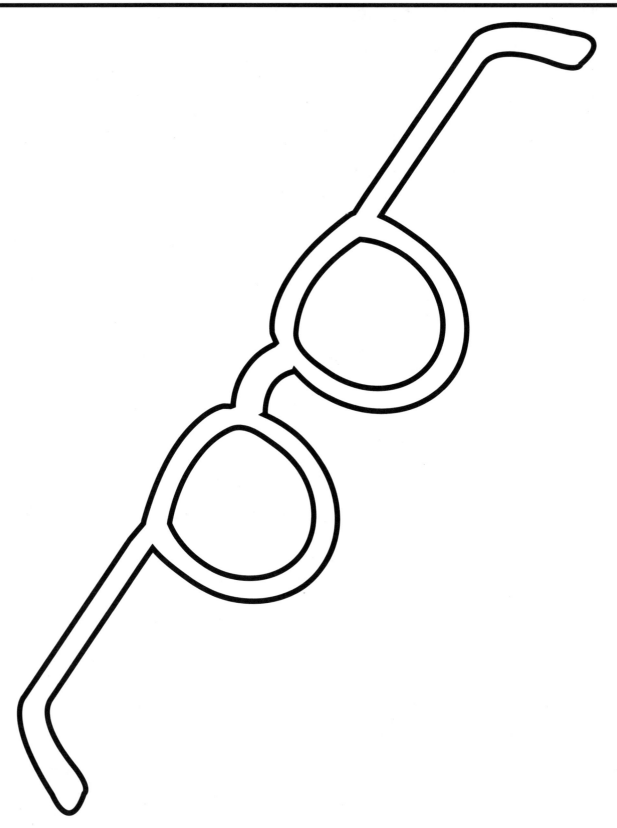

Jesus Calls Out Lazarus
John 11:1-45

MEMORY VERSE

"Lazarus, come out!"
~ John 11:43

WHAT YOU NEED

- page 90, duplicated
- heavy white paper or card stock
- crayons
- safety scissors
- tape

BEFORE CLASS

Duplicate a pattern page for each child onto heavy white paper or card stock. For younger preschoolers, cut out the bracelets. Make a sample craft to show the children.

WHAT TO DO

1. Introduce the lesson by telling the story from John 11:1-45. Say, **Jesus could even command the dead to come back to life.**
2. Show the children the sample craft.
3. Distribute a pattern page to each child.
4. Say the memory verse.
5. Have the children cut out the bracelets, and fold them on the dashed lines.
6. While the children color the bracelets, say, **Jesus helped His friend Lazarus. Jesus helps all His friends.**
7. Help the children form a circle with the bracelets and tape at the seam.
8. Encourage the children to wear one bracelet and give away the other two.

EXTRA TIME

Have the children make extra bracelets to give to another class in the building.

azarus died before Jesus got there. But Jesus called Lazarus out of the grave. Make friendship bracelets to remember that Jesus helped His friend.

Jesus is My Friend

Jesus is My Friend

 Jesus is My Friend

Jesus is My Friend

Jesus Heals a Crippled Woman
Luke 13:10-17

MEMORY VERSE

"Woman, you are set free."
~ Luke 13:12

Woman, you
are set free.
Luke 13:12

WHAT YOU NEED

- page 92, duplicated
- crayons
- safety scissors
- paper fasteners

BEFORE CLASS

Duplicate a pattern page for each child. You will need two paper fasteners per child. For younger children, cut out the two figure rectangles. Make a sample craft to show the children.

WHAT TO DO

1. Introduce the lesson by telling the story from Luke 13:10-17. Say, **Jesus can set us free from sickness, sadness and sins. Jesus loves us.**
2. Show the children the sample craft.
3. Distribute a pattern page to each child.
4. Say the memory verse.
5. Have the children cut the two rectangles from the page.
6. Help the children place the upper body of the woman over the marked X. Push a paper fastener through the X. Bend the fastener at the back.
7. Have the children glue the memory verse into the marked rectangle.
8. Allow the children to color the picture as time allows. Have the children move the woman to bend, then straighten up as you repeat the verse with them.

EXTRA TIME

Provide cotton swabs. Have the children glue cotton swabs around the edge of the picture to form a frame.

woman was all bent over. Jesus healed her, so she could stand tall and straight.

Woman, you are set free.
Luke 13:12

Jesus Healed Many People
Mark 1:32-34

MEMORY VERSE

Jesus healed many.
~ Mark 1:34

WHAT YOU NEED

- page 94, duplicated
- crayons

BEFORE CLASS

Duplicate a pattern page for each child.

WHAT TO DO

1. Introduce the lesson by telling the story from Mark 1:32-34.
2. Distribute a pattern page to each child.
3. Say the memory verse.
4. Encourage the children to help each sick person find the way to Jesus. Have the children color the pictures as time allows. Have the children color the pictures.

EXTRA TIME

Make a simple path by taping sheets of construction paper to the floor. Have the children find their way to Jesus by following the path. Make the game more difficult for older children by making two or three different colored paths that cross over each other. Tell the children to follow the "red" path, "purple" path or "blue" path.

Help the sick people find their way to Jesus. Jesus healed many people.